OUR ETERNITY

Our Eternity

BOOK OF 40 POEMS

Ja'Mir Parham

Copyright

Copyright © 2024 Jamir Parham
All Rights Reserved
No part of this publication may be reproduced, distributed or transmitted in any form or by any means, including photocopying recording, or other electronic or mechanical methods, without prior written permission from the author, except in the case of brief quotations embodied in critical reviews and certain other noncommercial uses permitted by copyright law. For permission requests, write to the author at:

Jamir Parham
P.O. Box 662
Henderson NC 27536
ISBN: 978-1-7378570-2-0
Library of Congress Control Number: 2024910373

Cover Photo inspired by @lutberbel
Special discounts are available on quantity purchases by corporations, associations, and others. For details, contact the author at:
Jamir Parham
www.jamirparham.com
parhamjamir4@gmail.com

Contents

Copyright — v
Introduction — xi
Dedication — xiii

One
What Do I Do? — 1

Two
Heaven's Gift To Me — 3

Three
The Color Brown — 6

Four
The Color I Wish Was Mine — 8

Five
The Senses I Have — 10

Six
Who Am I — 12

Seven
Silent Tears — 14

Eight
Death's Embrace — 16

Nine
The Crimson Rose   17

Ten
Vermillion   19

Eleven
A Man Beneath The Sky   21

Twelve
To Be The Poem And Not The Poet   23

Thirteen
Unforgotten Love   24

Fourteen
The Love I Give   26

Fifteen
Not You But I   28

Sixteen
The Letter I Should've Sent   30

Seventeen
The Siren's Song   31

Eighteen
A Thousand Miles For You   33

Nineteen
Across The World   35

Twenty
A Dying Star   37

Twenty-One
Amare's Absentia   38

Twenty-Two
What Riches Can Not Buy					39

Twenty-Three
Till Death Do Us Part					41

Twenty-Four
My Goodbye					43

Twenty-Five
A Door Not To Be Unlocked					44

Twenty-Six
When the Music Dies					46

Twenty-Seven
God's Fallen Son					47

Twenty-Eight
A Spider's Tears					49

Twenty-Nine
The Beauty From Afar					50

Thirty
To My First					52

Thirty-One
The King's Grace					54

Thirty-Two
A Mother's Son					56

Thirty-Three
My Roman Empire					58

Thirty-Four
A Lover's Scar					59

Thirty-Five
Our Promise   61

Thirty-Six
God's Answer   63

Thirty-Seven
To The Sister I Met Yesterday   65

Thirty-Eight
God's Architect   67

Thirty-Nine
Death and His Soldier   69

Forty
Adam's Wish   71

Acknowledgements   73
About The Author   74

Introduction

Why Do I Write?

There is beauty in breathing life onto an empty paper, turning miniscule words into an eloquent song of my conjuring. To write is to make art, an art with no bounds and no limitations. Wordplay is like knitting a sweater. Words are threads that need to be sewn together. In 10th grade, my counselor made a joke about me being an author because of how I articulate life; little did she know that I would make a poem just because of her comment.

I handed her my poem before homeroom and walked off. She grabbed me in the hallway later to tell me that she was at a loss of words. She cried with awe when she read it. I squealed with a smile reflecting the sun's rays. It was comforting to see my words not go unheard, and made me want to share again.

My poems are gifts of words to anyone willing to read as I share the words in my heart. Poetry allows me to open my heart and write the words I want to say, the words I never had the bravery to say as I begin to ride the wings of freedom. I am the "quiet kid" but poetry gives me a voice.

A story is meant to be told and I am learning to use my voice and tell my story through poetry. When I go about making a poem, I would think of a title spontaneously and start clapping like a maniac. From there, I just say what I got to say, something I never knew how to do.
  One day, I saw a spoken word:
  perfect cannot describe it. The wordplay,
  the command in her voice, the atmosphere,
  the tone, how
  she sped up…
  and slowed down.
It was a Love Jawn with Shay the Poet and she was breathtaking. The chemistry was unmatched and her performance left me stunned. This lady was knitting these words in such a manner that called to me, I heard my name and couldn't turn away. I was leaving Earth and began to land somewhere else; a place I never would have imagined. I had to try it for myself; I was a rocket ship ready to explode.

  Coming up with line by line, thread by thread with my needle to create a cozy sweater. A sweater of my design that I wear proudly. Knitting these sweaters has become me. It is the blood within my veins and the nerves alongside my brain.

Dedication

To the little child who didn't know where to go, lost without a heart. Look at how far you have grown and how far you have fallen to become the person we are today.

One

What Do I Do?

I don't know what to do
As I lie begging for a redo
To fly away
So time wouldn't pry
Where did they go
The friends for show
Even I want a hello
Though I know
I'm different
A cruel magnificence
How do I withdraw my flaws
That leaves me in awe
As it gnaws at my heart
For my crime at the start
Why was I punished at birth
I too am from the earth
A child from him in the sky
Then why?

Answer me why
I'm one of them?
Yet the only one condemned
Destined to be alone
The fact that whispers to my bones
What do I do
So this shall not remain true

Two

Heaven's Gift To Me

What is a gift?
A kind gesture
to create a shift,
igniting a smile
to overcome any trial
Can be simple words
forming a flying bird
Can be simple actions
causing a reaction as
bright as Michael Jackson
Heaven's gift to me
was a rose,
An unexpected nominee
With a big heart
and a face of art
Wild like fire
brimming with desire
Appealing attire

so elegant so intelligent,
Never not be relevant
Possessing a mother's kindness
A mother's touch, a mother's blindness
Coming in clutch
Looking smug
Thinking she's a thug but she doesn't have to be
Lay your feet, I want you to agree
There is safety in these sheets
Safety in these arms
No alarms in my gentle charm
A pretty girl, headstrong
A pretty pearl
So funny a sunny bunny
Collecting smiles like it's money
So much energy, so very kind
A brewing synergy
Putting my throat in a bind
Her words leave me speechless
A gentle voice
That'll never be reachless
Reaching into my heart
Fixing what was apart
She couldn't be more perfect
But she doesn't think she is
Worrying about retrospect
It's not a complex quiz
She's heaven gift
Meeting her was fateful

True and swift
I couldn't be more grateful

Three

The Color Brown

The Color Brown
Warm and vivid
Beyonce in town
With a crown
To lift our frowns
The color of the trees
Tall and towering
Flowing with the breeze
Holding the keys
Bringing me to an ease
The color of tea
Soothing and sweet
Such glee
Watching this DVD
It's quite the treat
The color of the ground
Always so profound
I don't need an ultrasound

It's in her hair
On her skin
It's everywhere
Given by our kin
Tears to repair
Humanity's sins
From a daring prayer
My pretty twin
With a grin on her chin
A win to spin
On how we begin
This beautiful mother
Strange yet assuring
Alluring and renown
A color like no other
The color brown

Four

The Color I Wish Was Mine

Baby Blue
The color of the skies
The color of her eyes
Heavens brew
A magical view
Seen from a shoe
Breaking taboo
As envy grew
Ocean's breeze
Keys to appease
But not guarantee
A dream
That'll never come to be
A sign from the divine
Lines to assign
Our varying designs

Craving to redefine
So that this color may be mine

Five

The Senses I Have

I have no eyes
Yet I see her smile
Such dazzling style
Many miles like the Nile
I have no ears
Yet I hear her voice
This perfect sphere
Which steer my fears
Without choice
Cheer and rejoice
I cannot speak
My throat is weak
But from a miracle
From the Greeks
On the tallest peaks
I found a shriek
This is not theoretical
When I looked at her

"How are you sir?"
It was a blur
What lacked became were
I have no nose
Yet I smell this rose
Which grows and pose
As the wind blows
When she arose I suppose
I cannot touch
Yet I can feel
This steel, this zeal
As she heal and steal
This old little eel
I have no senses
Yet I sense her presence
With no pretenses
This sweet fragrance
With no expenses and no defenses
I can sense
This dense door
This perfect score
I can sense even more

Six

Who Am I

Who am I
A person in the sky
One of many
A common penny
But who am I
Just standing by
High and dry
Trying to deny
My cry in July
But who am I
What can I gain
So simple and plain
Like the rain in a chain
Connected veins in one brain
Going insane playing
Confusing video games
Looking for a name
Placing blame

On a hurricane
But who am I
An imitated clone
Without one's own phone
An unmoving stone
A cone in the zone
Thrown and blown
By a cyclone
Flown into the unknown
But who am I
Who are you
Not to pry
But what is true
What is the answer
To this distant cancer

Seven

Silent Tears

My pretty handsome boy
The golden boy
With promise
Full of joy
But someone's ploy
Who is he?
Someone's tool
To never be free?
Under rule
In a duel
With his mind
Eyes to blind
To remind what's unwind
Tears behind his smile
Hiding his trials with style
Tears with no sound
The crowned prince
Never found, always frowned

No one hears his tears
The growing peers
Spiraling spheres
With haunting fears
Aging years
With Silent Tears

Eight

Death's Embrace

A lover's kiss
A mother's touch
Giving dismiss
Our loving crutch
Her words reassuring
Letting us rest
No longer enduring
For we tried our best
Kind and warm
Soft and gentle
Unlike the norm
Very sentimental
Closing the curtain
Ending life's race
Lifting the burden
Death's Embrace

Nine

The Crimson Rose

A beautiful flower
A bright fiery red
The color of love
The color of passion
A fateful thread
Bloomed in darkness
Born of compassion
Dark and rich
A light from above
Shining and brilliant
A fitting glove
Such elegance
So may elements
This beautiful flower
One of a kind
Born of light

Beautifully designed
How should I propose
To the Crimson Rose

Ten

Vermillion

Visually Striking
A daring spiking
Brave and forward
Truly noward
Pertains its beauty
No belonging duty
Wild and fierce
A bewildering pierce
Surprisingly gentle
Beautiful dentil
Fiery love
Unfitting gloves
Rare and unique
Could never be bleak
Dressed in fashion
With a burning passion
The rising phoenix
The defying helix

Free in the skies
Drums of liberation
Eyes on the prize
One of our imagination

Eleven

A Man Beneath The Sky

Why am I up here you ask
Well, there's nowhere else to go
Even these words
Are rejoicing to leave
Smiles brush my arms
Yet somehow worlds away
I alone am what is left
Just me and the sky
An audience with no display
Flowers left in the dirt
Growing without purpose
Bear witness
To the man without a heart
Scarred by the one above
Who abandoned his humanity
Foolish. He was never of them
Even as they lied that he was
"Abandoning" the home he never visited

Endless were his thoughts in the sky
Conflicted with what was and what will
But the clouds warm his solitude
With a blanket of rain
Made of his tear's silk
Even he can cry
The inhuman bastard
Once a boy
Just a man beneath the sky
Peering unto his soul
Until he no longer can

Twelve

To Be The Poem And Not The Poet

Oh to be the poem and not the poet
Oh to be pursued not just pursuing
Giving his all in tribute
With nothing else to contribute
Oh to be loved not just loving
A love that is embraced and returned
I thought I've earned
Oh how it burns!
This pain in my chest
Stirring in my breasts
My soul is not at rest
All that is left
A request that hasn't been assessed
Haven't I been blessed?
Now read from bottom to top

Thirteen

Unforgotten Love

So much so full
Strong as a bull
Life springing
Leaving me grinning
Unabridged light
Endless height
Grown and kept
Won't neglect
Embers of passion
Once satisfaction
Now disarrayed
Not displayed
Still cherish
Tasteful relish
Not forgotten
Stay like cotton
Still I love
The unretained dove

Doesn't remember
No such rember
The echoes of joy
Abaft now croy

Fourteen

The Love I Give

The Love I Give
Is beautiful and bright
Small but mighty
Cherished and in bloom
Growing tasteful fruit
Keeping you warm and safe
Arms to hold you
A hand to brush
Food to nourish
And clothes to wear
Treasure to behold
A golden sphere
Uncostly but priceless
Giving directions
To guide in life
A fire to heal

Given without request
Even if unwanted
That is the love I give

Fifteen

Not You But I

Not you but I
Has forgotten the summer day
The crimson sun
Shining the clouds
Feeding the roses
Watering the pansies
Not you but I
Has forgotten the breeze
Carrying dreams
Lifting hearts
Not you but I
Has forgotten promises
Of newfound love
Strong and fierce
Bright in fever
Not you but I
Feels loss and guilt
Once filled before

Reminiscing the once possessed
Not you but I who has forgotten
But remembers too late

Sixteen

The Letter I Should've Sent

You being here
My heart wishes for
But you don't
I've done wrong
You should hate me
Why do you love me?
Answer my question
But before you do
Go away
Now read it from bottom to top

Seventeen

The Siren's Song

A beautiful melancholy
Short and sweet
Promising temptation
Gracing my ears
With glistening tunes
Dressed in fashion
Freshly tailored
In close inspection
Tattered in rags
Frumpish and dumpish
Silent but luring
A drowning death
Looming ahead
No such treasure
But lead instead

The Siren's Song is a song used by sirens to lure sailors to their death, just because something looks good, sounds good, or may even smell good, doesn't necessarily means it is good for you. The Siren's Song is the most beautiful song you'll ever hear but it could also be the last song you'd ever hear if you do.

Eighteen

A Thousand Miles For You

The rose that grew
Hiding a Jew
Wanting to sprout
Despite life's drought
Withholding doubt
Towering mountains with
Drowning seas
Scarce fountains and killing disease
My unwavering loyalty
All for you
Supreme royalty never in review
Forever unchanging, still remaining
Facing tyrant's paintings
Already in trials
No need for exchanging
A thousand miles

Through storm and fury
Smiles and joy
Embracing purely
All of Troy
A thousand miles
The length I'll do
Approaching each tile
All for you

Nineteen

Across The World

Fever runs
Golden suns
Exploding guns
Within my lungs
Kisses blown
Calls on the phone
As love is honed
My heart is cloned
No longer mine
Both combined
Dripping wine
Lives intertwined
Miles apart
Unsweetened tart
As small darts
Are thrown on the chart
A dying start
But must restart

It must go on
The future is upon
Hope is spawned
Doubt shall scatter
Nothing else matters
I have you
That's our cue
From across the world

Twenty

A Dying Star

Once young and bright
Fearful of the earth
High above the clouds
Beaming with grace
Holding its heart
In open hands
Now falling from the heavens
Plunging into desolace
Losing his smile
Drowning in sorrow
In a lonely castle
Lies a dying star

Twenty-One

Amare's Absentia

To the night we met
Under the crescent moon
In fate's weaving net
Lives were strewn
Heaven's stellar light
Innocence's reflection
Burning the night
With a cunning misdirection
Where did it go?
The archer's arrow
All for show
Our chance was narrow
Maybe if thy turn back time
It shall land on the dime

Twenty-Two

What Riches Can Not Buy

What good is for a man
to gain the world yet lose his soul
What is to be gained
by reigning the unchained
Condemning the heart
to a cage for minimum wage
Riches cannot buy Heaven's scroll to man,
but swallowing coal all for a goal
is how sin began
Rivers of gold are not enough
To unfold the stories waiting to be told
As greed's wile cannot steal life's smile
A gift cannot be bought
only to be given not sought
It wouldn't be a gift if it could

As time flies by, forced to say goodbye
You will realize in adulthood
What riches cannot buy

Twenty-Three

Till Death Do Us Part

The words I said to you
They grew
Yet flowers never bloomed
A future now entombed
By a love I once groomed
With my soul's perfume
When did our July
Become the memory
That I deny
Our words lost in the sky
Finalizing our goodbye
It is still here
In my heart
The frontier of our career
Wishing to restart
To when promises weren't lies
But the prize that the ally
In the skies comprised

Yet I still allow
The vow we made
To be the blade in plough
"Till Death Do Us Part"
The words that drove us apart.

Twenty-Four

My Goodbye

My goodbye, spoken with regret. I repay my debt
Remembering the sun, recalling our fun
Our late-night calls, Our trips to the malls
The smiles we shared, The love we declared
Under the frosted moon, In the afternoon
The show came to a close
Frozen was my rose
Crippled, a dying prime
I borrowed time
On the road driven
What was given
Shall return
The fruits cherished now burned
Whispering their tears
Shouting their fears on dead ears
Words from the sky
My cry, my goodbye

Twenty-Five

A Door Not To Be Unlocked

Bloody. Ravaged. Where do I begin?
Disaster, the blade carried by the wind
Unleashed upon the night.
A palace of beauty turned to ruin.
What did I do?
To earn God's fury as he strike the love
That I groomed with my heart's perfume.
My precious love; the world on a pedestal,
Helpless to Orpheus's lyre
Blind to a musician's love
Vanished without a glance
Abandoning the throne I delicately crafted.
"Never open the door for a stranger"
A lesson foolishness doesn't adhere
But is it foolish to be a child?
Birthed with a heart of daisies

Victims for the streets of London
A gift not to be opened
A door not to be unlocked.
Yet I was a child, a foolish one at that.

Twenty-Six

When the Music Dies

When the music dies
The curtains close
The crowd array
The show is over
There isn't a reason to stay
But I wish someone would.
On stage was Spiderman
Yet now is Peter Parker
The common man
The celebrity walks past
Trampled on for the main event
"We love you"
No you don't
When the music dies
So do the lies they tell
The smile was for the audience
The mask they all believe
Lacking the glasses to see what's there

Twenty-Seven

God's Fallen Son

God's Fallen Son
Where do I even begin?
I can't find the words
That are lost in the wind
Shadows hide in fear
Even the rain fails to appear
Leaving hell's fire as my peer
What is a king
Without a throne
Who stands alone
Surrounded by stones
I was only a kid
When my heart was undid
Cursed with darkness
That pushes all with its sharpness
how heartless of God
To abandon the odd with just a nod
An empty wallet

Is all that I own
Not enough for his love
For I have been disowned.

Twenty-Eight

A Spider's Tears

Oh to be a butterfly
Lost in the sky
Tasting the clouds
Performing for the crowd
While I remain on the deserted ship
A lonely spider
With his wings clipped
The unwanted outsider
Disgusting. Ugly
With a glass of cider
Why so distrusting?
Its humanity's DNA
To hate their prey
What must I do to deserve their love
Threads of a fitting glove
As I am beautiful
It is indisputable

Twenty-Nine

The Beauty From Afar

A crystal pair of eyes
Filled with a prize
That's just the right size
a surprise in those thighs
That I cannot deny
Hips that dip
Equipped with a whip
But those plush lips
Makes my heart skip
Dare she have the gall
To tear down China's walls
Like the stalls at the mall
Starting to remodel
My heart's bottle
Because of Vogue's model
Just at the sight of her
I could write a novel

She is truly beautiful
One of a kind
A beauty of fine wine
It is indisputable
Truly sublime are the lines beyond my confines
On par with a superstar
The beauty from afar
This beautiful star

Thirty

To My First

To my First,
Words cannot express
My sorrow for our
Begotten tales
Our precious fruits
Bearing youth's innocence
Spoiled to contamination
A dream's nightmare
A paradise that I culled
A child's first dessert
It was everything
The wife that never came to be
The queen without a ring
Does your heart recall the past
Even though it does not beat
Can a heart still break
Even if it already has
Little did I know

Our hearts were entwined
I have killed us both
My First and my Last
And for that
I apologize.

Thirty-One

The King's Grace

The heavens did not reach his shoulders
The skies were his soldiers
His steps shook the earth
Even nature knew his worth
A king amongst kings
Fate couldn't touch his life's string
Always the first into battle
We weren't his cattle
We were his children
Kept far away from Evil's prison
What father sends his child to die
Only parting with a goodbye
And into battle he rode
Bucephalus onto Morningstar's road
An angel of death
Eating souls' breath
His sword called for no mercy
Yet he was kinder than Percy

The night-time star
No wonder he was so bizarre
But he was my father
And none shall dare to dishonor
All hail the King's Grace
For he has beaten God's race

Thirty-Two

A Mother's Son

How far have I fallen
A king without a castle
Was I truly a king
The world laid on my shoulders
Wine flowed beneath my sword
The heavens have trembled at my name
But what makes a king?
Death was my right hand
While solitude as my left
But why?
To make her proud
What was her name?
The mother that I never knew
To ring the great bells
To obtain greatness
 It was the child's dream to make her smile
A smile that dwarfed the sun
Where did it go?

I have failed
The child without a face, without a name
I'm sorry little one
I wasn't good enough
We were meant to be great
We were meant to be beautiful
The savior of dreams
But I became a monster instead

Thirty-Three

My Roman Empire

My Roman Empire was when she walked away
The mom that he gained just for today
My Roman Empire was when she knitted her threads
The little girl that wove the heart he wears to bed
My Roman Empire was when she hugged me
A mother's arms set Cain free
My Roman Empire was when she abandoned us
The little boy fussed but there was nothing to discuss
My Roman Empire was when she read his poem
She valued his precious totem
My Roman Empire was when she listened
With every word, the stars in her eyes glistened
Regardless whether they go or stay
My Roman Empire is those that have seen my life's essay.

Thirty-Four

A Lover's Scar

"I was only 17"
Yet so was I
We were children
Is it a sin
To be a child
To be drunk on love
And the fruits of passion
Orpheus promised
The archer's arrow struck
Raining tears of love
Or so I thought
A dessert to my ears
That my heart savored
It was everything
The treasures that reality did not bring
The wishes that I dreamt
But every dream has its end
Every child has to grow up

To face God's cruel illusion
Of the rose that never bloomed
But oh how it wished
Placing a scar
On its fragile heart

Thirty-Five

Our Promise

She promised that she would stay
God put her to the test
We argued over the laundry
Thunder roared in the house
Lightning's rage streaked in her eyes
I thought she would run away
But she didn't
She pinched my cheeks with a kiss
I forgot to text her
Loneliness did in my stead
It occupied her room
Filled her lungs
I thought she'd text someone else
But she didn't
She waited and battled the winter's chill
Only with a blanket till the sun rose
She needed help with homework
But I didn't have the time

I'd thought she'd give up
On the husband that was never there
But she didn't
She greeted me with math
and watched my struggle with Einstein
With a torturous smile
One day I worked a little too late
I thought she'd be home
She always was
But she wasn't
I wasn't fast enough to chain her wings
She broke our promise
But I did first
I wasn't there, I didn't do my best
So God put our promise to rest

Thirty-Six

God's Answer

You cannot find the words
For I have them here
The wind was blown by them
And so was I
My precious son
The chosen one
Compared to none
You fell from grace
I wanted you to embrace your place
The fire's silence was for you to atone
A king isn't of his throne
But of the surrounding stones
Low as they may be
But as beautiful and as high as we
The brightest star
Blinded by darkness
But your wicked sharpness
Keeps you afar

You are welcome anytime
Pass me the cigar
Look behind those scars
And see what I have in store
I have not abandoned you
My love is at the door

Thirty-Seven

To The Sister I Met Yesterday

To the sister I met Yesterday
How dare you
Come out the blue
High and mighty
Larger than life
Plucking the knife from my hand
With a smile
Solitude has become my sword
Yet you disarmed me despite its edge
"How beautiful you are"
How dare you
Pluck the child from my heart's prison
And give him a hug
Picking him up with a mother's love
Your words became his first dessert
The gall to tear down these walls

Without my permission.
Thank you
For the gift I always wanted
But too proud to admit

Thirty-Eight

God's Architect

How splendid you are
As you wield the stars
To create my gifts
That never fails
To lift my spirit's shifts
You don't always get a medal
As you give life to metal
But the batter doesn't matter
Rather the success of each chapter
Like your creation
Be unyielding, soar to your imagination
Like your hair
Ride wind's freedom
And don't give a care
Laugh my child
I'm quite proud

And with that she smiled
As her heart beat loud
And yet it was allowed

Thirty-Nine

Death and His Soldier

Become my blade
So I can taste their lives
Your debt shall go unpaid
Unless you caress the knives
As old as time
Such are your crimes
Yet you run from them
Cowardly.
Expected of your kind
As greed leads the blind
Only to end with me
The arbiter's decree
My lucky date
That forgets to pay
But cries and prays
When followed by the sea
I am here
What will you do

When death is near
And blood's wine is due
Pay what's mine
Now or later
That is the creator's fine

Forty

Adam's Wish

Fallen from paradise
From a snake's advice
My precious Adam
Held by evil's vice
Yet *He* punished him
To stop evil's might
To prevent weeds in the garden
But was it right?
he loved his father
What son shouldn't?
he wanted to be like his dad
Even if he couldn't
Which made the boy mad
Mad with himself
But sad in his heart
As his arms couldn't
Reach *His* divine art
The boy, made a man

But only just a man
Unlike his father
His biggest fan
To not be dismissed
Was his only wish

Acknowledgements

Despite being the author, this book isn't of my creation but the creation of all those who have come into my life no matter how brief or how long they have stayed. However, I do have to acknowledge my editor, publisher, and my favorite aunt, Ulaonda Parham, for her vision and guiding me to my very own book. She has refined my drafts into a polished and beautiful work. To Breeana White and Antonique Spence, thank you for supporting me when I felt like the world was ending and helping me find my passion in writing. To Connor Yarborough (the smartest guy I know), thank you for being one of my best friends. You have read almost every poem I have made and critiqued them allowing me to take them to the next level. My poetry has grown so much due to your words and contribution. This book wouldn't have been possible without these individuals and more, but I'll be here all day listing all the names though I am grateful for all that have helped me in any shape or form. And finally, thank you to all that have read my book for being a witness to my life's story.

About The Author

Ja'Mir Parham

Ja'Mir Parham is a high school senior set to embark on his college journey at Elon University. He stands out as an Odyssey Scholar with a dual passion for physics and creative writing. He loves science and philosophy; always questioning the world around him but what truly rules his heart is romance stories which is where his mind runs wild like the child he still is.

www.ingramcontent.com/pod-product-compliance
Lightning Source LLC
Chambersburg PA
CBHW030558080526
44585CB00012B/414